Acknowledgements

The author would like to thank Erika Evans for her help and support during the writing and production of this publication.

Mark Evans has been a teacher for over 25 years. He has taught in Australia, Japan, Malaysia and the UK. He graduated in languages from University College London and has a PGCE, CELTA, DELTA, Diploma in ESOL, as well as an MA in English Language Teaching. He currently lives in London where he teaches at a college and a university.

This edition published in London, England in 2021

ISBN: 9798543021309

Text copyright @2021, Mark Evans

No part of this book may be reproduced in any form, or by any means, without prior permission in writing from the author.

MeEducation

Please feel free to contact the author at - meeducation@yahoo.com

Visit the website at **https://meeducation.net**

Also by the same author:

- *Pre Entry Grammar*
- *Entry 2 Grammar*
- *Entry 3 Grammar*
- *Level 1 Grammar*
- *Level 2 Grammar*
- *Pre Entry English*
- *Entry 1 Reading and Writing*
- *Entry 2 Reading and Writing*
- *Entry 3 Reading and Writing*
- *Level 1 Reading and Writing*
- *Level 2 Reading and Writing*
- *Easy English*
- *English for Work*

YouTube ESOL King

Table of Contents

Be Verb Positive...	5
Be Verb Negative..	7
My Friend...	9
Be Verb Speaking Practice....................................	10
Common Mistakes: Be Verb...................................	11
Have/has – Positive	12
Have/has – Negative	14
Common Mistakes: Have..	15
Possessives..	17
Can/Can't...	18
Can you?..	19
Can/Can't Reading: The Smith Family.....................	22
Can/Can't Speaking Practice..................................	23
Can Crossword...	25
Common Mistakes: Can/Can't................................	26
My Family's Likes and Dislikes...............................	27
Do you like?...	28
Like/Don't Like Speaking Practice...........................	30
Common Mistakes: Like/Don't Like.........................	31
Present Simple...	33
Derek's Day...	34
Present Simple Speaking Practice...........................	35
Danny's Day..	35
Present Simple Crossword.....................................	37
Present Simple Mistakes.......................................	38
Present Continuous..	39

Present Continuous Speaking Practice	40
Present Continuous Crossword	42
Present Continuous Errors	43
Past Tense Regular	44
Past Regular: Negative and Questions	45
Did/Didn't	47
Dahira's Dinner	49
Past Regular Speaking Practice	50
Common Mistakes: Past Tense Regular	51
Be Verb Past Positive	52
Be Verb Past Negative	54
Was/Were Speaking Practice	56
Common Mistakes: Was/Were	57
Past Irregular	58
William's Weekend	61
Past Irregular Speaking Practice	62
Past Tense Crossword	63
Common Mistakes: Past Irregular	64
Question Forms	65
Future Plans – Going to	67
Going to – short answers	68
William's Weekend Work	69
Going to Speaking Practice	70
Going to Crossword	72
Common Mistakes: Going to	73
Answer Key	74

"Be" Verb - Positive

Copy the "be" verb into the box

I am	
You are	
He is	
She is	
It is	
We are	
They are	

Write the correct form of the "be" verb:

1) They _____ kind.

2) We _____ very happy.

3) The road _____ short.

4) You _____ very fast.

5) He _____ a nice man.

6) I _____ from Spain.

7) The coffee _____ hot.

8) I _____ 45 years old.

9) My class _____ fun.

10) Sally and Sarah _____ tired.

11) I _____ very sick today.

12) Bill _____ tall.

13) My father _____ big.

14) The food _____ good.

15) Edward _____ fat.

16) It _____ sunny today.

17) I _____ a cleaner.

18) The UK _____ cold.

19) We _____ very late.

20) My trousers _____ new.

Writing Practice

*Write 5 sentences using **am**:*

1) ....

2) ....

3) ....

4) ....

5) ....

*Write 5 sentences using **is**:*

1) ....

2) ....

3) ....

4) ....

5) ....

*Write 5 sentences using **are**:*

1) ....

2) ....

3) ....

4) ....

5) ....

"Be" Verb - Negative

Copy the "be" verb into the box

I am not	
You are not	
He is not	
She is not	
It is not	
We are not	
They are not	

Write the correct negative form of the "be" verb:

1) We _____ sad.

2) The men _____ nice.

3) The teacher _____ tall.

4) She _____ Italian.

5) Mary _____ slim.

6) I _____ from this country.

7) It _____ a nice day.

8) The restaurant _____ good.

9) My country _____ hot.

10) His trousers _____ clean.

11) The weather _____ hot.

12) The road _____ short.

13) I _____ sick today.

14) I _____ 20 years old.

15) I _____ a teacher.

16) My friends _____ here.

17) You _____ slow.

18) They _____ late.

19) Fred and Gary _____ slow.

20) Her jacket _____ new.

Writing Practice

*Write 5 sentences using **am not**:*

1) ....

2) ....

3) ....

4) ....

5) ....

*Write 5 sentences using **is not**:*

1) ....

2) ....

3) ....

4) ....

5) ....

*Write 5 sentences using **are not**:*

1) ....

2) ....

3) ....

4) ....

5) ....

My Friend

My friend's name is Adam. He is 35 year old. He is from Poland. He is very tall. He is a waiter in a restaurant in a big hotel. His hobby is swimming. He is a very happy man.

Adam is married. His wife's name is Mary. She isn't from Poland. She is from Scotland. She is a childminder. Her hobby is running. She is a happy woman. They have two children. Their names are Ana and Maria. Ana is 7 years old and Maria is 10 years old. They are pupils at a school in their town. They like their school very much.

1) How old is Adam?

2) What is his job?

3) What is his hobby?

4) Is he happy?

5) What is Adam's wife's name?

6) Is she from Poland?

7) What is her job?

8) What are their children's names?

9) How old are the children?

10) Where are they pupils?

Extension – write at least 3 more questions about the text:

Be Verb Speaking Practice

1) is/your/name/what?

2) you/happy/are/today?

3) hobby/your/what/is?

4) you/are/married?

5) your/address/what/is?

6) job/is/what/your?

7) today/how/is/the/weather?

8) you/are/now/hungry?

9) your/favourite/food/is/what?

10) drink/what/your/is/favourite?

11) your/country's/what/name/is?

12) friend/who/is/your/best?

13) your/friends'/names/what/are?

14) your/friends/where/are/now?

Extension – mark at least 5 more questions to ask your partner:

Common Mistakes – Be Verb

Find the mistakes in these sentences and write the correct version below:

1) I no is happy.

....

2) John are a nice man.

....

3) Is you busy today?

....

4) I is a very lucky woman.

....

5) My favourite food are pizza.

....

6) My teacher is sick today?

....

7) I no am late because I took the bus.

....

8) Simon he is very hungry.

....

9) I no am tired today.

....

10) They is my friends.

....

11) Tom and Sarah is nice people.

....

12) We is always nice to people.

....

Have/has - Positive

Copy the "have" verb into the box

I have	
You have	
He has	
She has	
It has	
We have	
They have	

Write the correct form of the "have" verb:

1) Ben _____ a pain in his leg.

2) We _____ a good teacher.

3) I _____ a ring.

4) I _____ no money today.

5) I _____ a new jacket.

6) You _____ nice hair.

7) I _____ a phone.

8) My country _____ many people.

9) Alex _____ fun.

10) Simon and Jack _____ a kind mother.

11) The car _____ a radio.

12) They _____ books.

13) Maggie _____ pens.

14) It _____ a tree.

15) He _____ a nice bike.

16) John _____ a hat.

17) We _____ new clothes.

18) My flat _____ a TV.

19) Dahira _____ a nice smile.

20) The restaurant _____ a good chef.

Writing Practice

*Write 10 sentences using **have**:*

1) ....

2) ....

3) ....

4) ....

5) ....

6) ....

7) ....

8) ....

9) ....

10) ....

*Write 10 sentences using **has**:*

1) ....

2) ....

3) ....

4) ....

5) ....

6) ....

7) ....

8) ....

9) ....

10) ....

Have/has - Negative

Copy the negative "have" verb into the box

I don't have	
You don't have	
He doesn't have	
She doesn't have	
It doesn't have	
We don't have	
They don't have	

Write the correct negative form of the "have" verb:

1) He _____ a fast car.

2) We _____ a pen.

3) The cat _____ fish.

4) They _____ books.

5) I _____ a house.

6) It _____ a small table.

7) I _____ time.

8) You _____ a cat.

9) The house _____ a big window.

10) Kim and Kelly _____ a garden.

11) I _____ an apple.

12) Rick _____ money.

13) Jim _____ a dog.

14) It _____ doors.

15) Dee _____ a rubber.

16) I _____ a book.

17) We _____ friends.

18) The UK _____ good weather.

19) Nick _____ a job.

20) Ben _____ a nice hat.

Writing Practice

*Write 10 sentences using **don't have**:*

1) ....

2) ....

3) ....

4) ....

5) ....

6) ....

7) ....

8) ....

9) ....

10) ....

*Write 10 sentences using **doesn't have**:*

1) ....

2) ....

3) ....

4) ....

5) ....

6) ....

7) ....

8) ....

9) ....

10) ....

Common Mistakes – Have

Find the mistakes in these sentences and write the correct version below:

1) He have a nice car.

....

2) We no have time to meet you today.

....

3) You do have the time?

....

4) She have long, black hair.

....

5) Ben and Billy has new books.

....

6) I has a nice teacher.

....

7) I no have much money in my pocket.

....

8) William he have a big house.

....

9) You no have new shoes.

....

10) We has a party at my house tomorrow.

....

11) My mother have very nice friends.

....

12) Ron no have a brother.

....

Possessives

Copy the possessives into the box:

Subject	Possessive	Possessive
I	My	
You	Your	
He	His	
She	Her	
It	Its	
We	Our	
They	Their	

Put the correct possessive into the gaps:

1) I like _____ friend very much.

2) She saw _____ next door neighbour in the supermarket.

3) Can I borrow _____ black pen, please?

4) We don't have _____ pens today so we can't write.

5) Mr and Mrs Jones are sad because they lost _____ cat yesterday.

6) Elizabeth loves _____ husband very much.

7) The dogs is licking _____ paws because they are dirty.

8) My dad is driving _____ new car around the town.

9) She went to visit _____ best friend at her new flat.

10) Sarah was late this morning because she missed _____ bus.

11) I like _____ school very much. I never miss a lesson.

12) My mother feeds _____ goldfish in the garden every day.

Can/Can't

Positive +		Negative -		Question ?	
I		I			I + infinitive?
You		You			you + infinitive?
He		He			he + infinitive?
She	can + infinitive	She	can't + infinitive	Can/ Can't	she + infinitive?
It		It			it + infinitive?
We		We			we + infinitive?
They		They			they + infinitive?

Write 6 things you can do:

1)..

2)..

3)..

4)..

5)..

6)..

Write 6 things you can't do:

1)..

2)..

3)..

4)..

5)..

6)..

Can you...?

| Can you _____ ? → Yes, I can. |
| → No, I can't. |

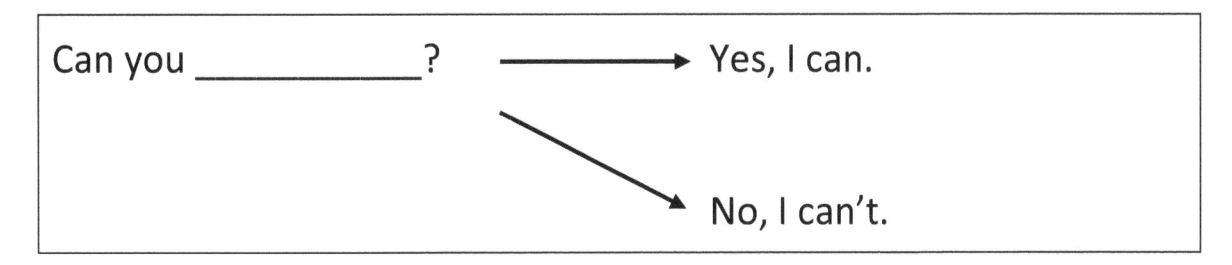

*Ask your partner these questions and **circle** their answers:*

Can you...

speak English?	Yes, I can.	No, I can't.
drive a car?	Yes, I can.	No, I can't.
ride a bike?	Yes, I can.	No, I can't.
cook?	Yes, I can.	No, I can't.
swim?	Yes, I can.	No, I can't.
dance?	Yes, I can.	No, I can't.
sing?	Yes, I can.	No, I can't.
climb a mountain?	Yes, I can.	No, I can't.
speak Arabic?	Yes, I can.	No, I can't.
play the guitar?	Yes, I can.	No, I can't.
draw?	Yes, I can.	No, I can't.
run fast?	Yes, I can.	No, I can't.
play football?	Yes, I can.	No, I can't.
use a computer?	Yes, I can.	No, I can't.

Extension – make more questions to ask your partner:

Writing Practice

*Write 8 things that your partner **can** do:*

1) He/She can..

2) ....

3) ....

4) ....

5) ....

6) ....

7) ....

8) ....

*Write 8 things that your partner **can't** do:*

1) He/She can't..

2) ....

3) ....

4) ....

5) ....

6) ....

7) ....

8) ....

Put "can" or "can't" in the spaces below:

1) From my bedroom window I _____ see a lovely park.

2) Sarah _____ exercise today because she has a bad headache.

3) My mother _____ ride a bike but she can't drive a car.

4) Peter _____ speak Spanish but he wants to learn.

5) Molly _____ dance very well because she has dance lessons.

6) _____ you help me open the door, please?

7) Alex _____ play the piano but he can play the guitar very well.

8) I _____ get to school on time if I take the bus.

9) I _____ play football well. I train every day.

10) Ana _____ speak French very well because she is from France.

11) I'm sorry but I _____ come to class today because I am sick.

12) Hi there! _____ you hear me now?

13) We _____ visit our friend today because my mother said we can't.

14) Why _____ you drive a car?

15) _____ you understand me when I speak English?

16) Arthur _____ go to work today because he has a bad cold.

17) Lily _____ sing beautifully. She has a private teacher.

18) I _____ play tennis very well. I am a member of a club.

*Extension - write at least 5 more sentences with **can/can't**:*

Can/Can't Reading: The Smith Family

John and Mary Smith are married with two children, Andrew and Maria. The Smith family can do many things.

John Smith can do many sports. He can play tennis, he can play football and he can play rugby. He can also swim very far. But he can't cook!

Mary Smith can cook very well. She can cook pasta, she can cook fish and she can cook meat. She can make delicious bread and she can make tasty salads. But she can't paint or draw.

Andrew Smith is good at art. He can paint beautiful pictures. He can draw cartoons and can write great stories. But he can't play a musical instrument.

Maria Smith is very good at music. She can play the piano, she can play the guitar and she can play the violin. She can sing very well but she can't dance.

1) How many people are there in the Smith family?

2) Who can do many sports?

3) Who can't cook?

4) What can Mary cook?

5) What is Andrew good at?

6) Can Andrew paint?

7) What can't Andrew do?

8) How many instruments can Maria play?

9) How well can Maria sing?

10) Can Maria dance?

Extension – make at least 3 more questions about the text:

1) ....

2) ....

3) ....

Can/Can't Speaking Practice

Put the words in order to make questions. Next ask your partner and add something extra:

1) you/drive/car/a/can?

2) bicycle/you/can/a/ride?

3) cook/can/you/best/what?

4) you/can/play/chess?

5) you/can/swim/well?

6) sport/what/you/can/best/do?

7) instrument/you/can/play/musical/a?

8) what/speak/you/can/languages?

9) far/how/you/can/run?

10) long/how/sleep/you/can?

11) picture/you/paint/a/draw/or/can?

12) you/how/can/English/practise/your?

13) sing/you/can/or/well/dance?

14) home/you/your/see/what/from/in/window/can/your?

Extension – write at least 5 more questions to ask your partner:

Writing Practice

*Write 10 sentences using **can**:*

1) ....

2) ....

3) ....

4) ....

5) ....

6) ....

7) ....

8) ....

9) ....

10) ....

*Write 10 sentences using **can't**:*

1) ....

2) ....

3) ....

4) ....

5) ....

6) ....

7) ....

8) ....

9) ....

10) ....

Can Crossword

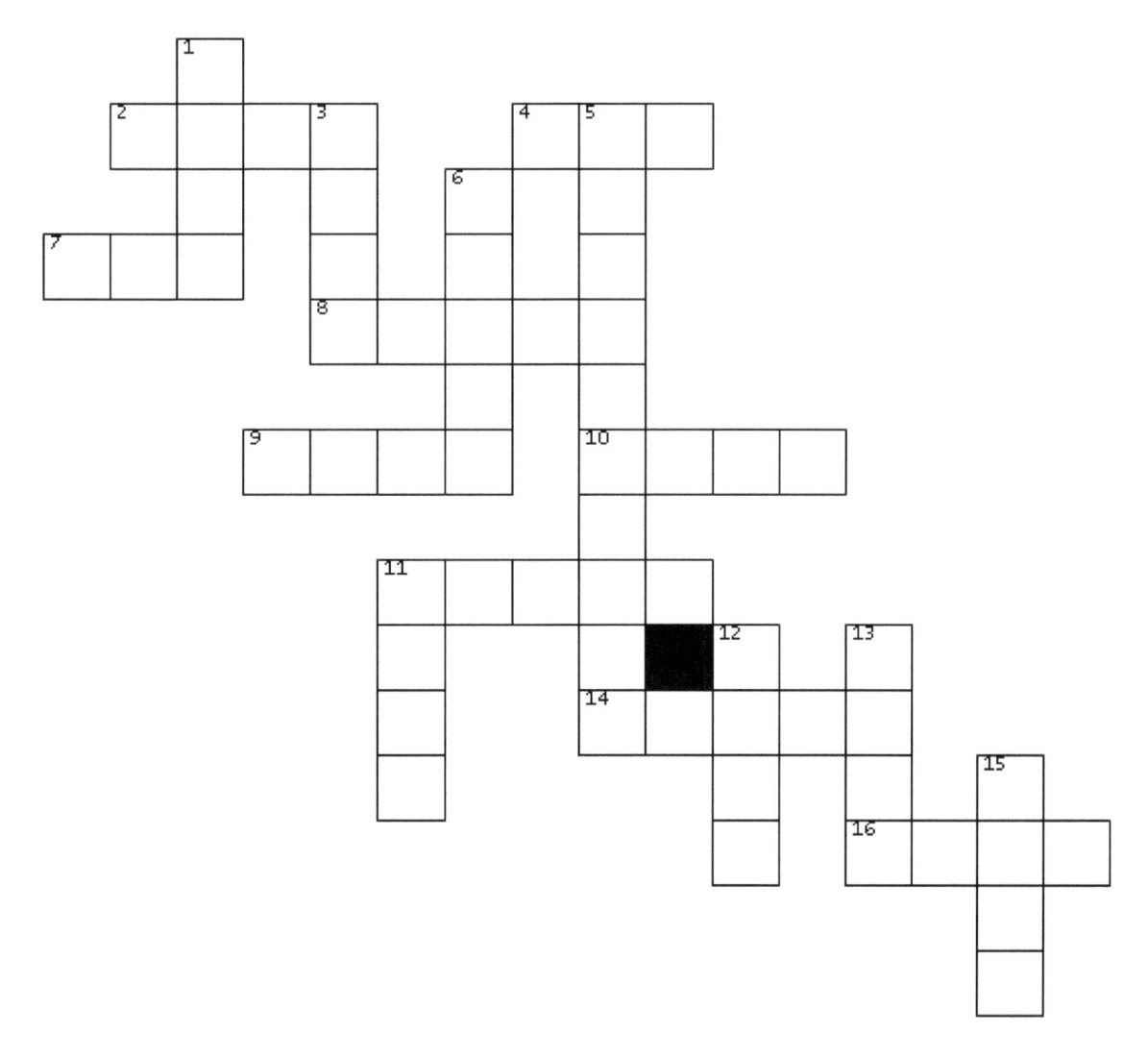

ACROSS
2. I can't _____ Chinese.
4. He can _____ fast.
7. Ann can't _____ home because she is too busy.
8. He can _____ a letter.
9. Benny can't _____ because he is sick.
10. I can _____ a beautiful song.
11. I can _____ French.
14. Can you _____ a car?
16. She can _____ the piano.

DOWN
1. Can you _____ me tomorrow?
3. She can _____ a nice picture.
5. Can you _____ me?
6. I can't _____ wine. It makes me sick.
11. Deanna can _____ in the sea.
12. Carina can _____ a bike.
13. Can you _____ me?
15. I can't _____ you as my phone is broken.

Common Mistakes – Can/Can't

Find the mistakes in these sentences and write the correct version below:

1) We can running in the park.

....

2) Linda no can dance.

....

3) You can help my friend?

....

4) She cans play the piano.

....

5) He is can driving a car.

....

6) I can no understanding you.

....

7) She can sings and dances beautifully.

....

8) You can use a computer?

....

9) I cant coming to class today because I am sick.

....

10) She can't listening to music because her radio is broken.

....

11) You can give me your rubber, please?

....

12) It is raining so we no can't go to the park.

....

My family's Likes and Dislikes

My family likes food very much but we all like different food. For vegetables, I like potatoes, carrots and broccoli but I don't like mushrooms or runner beans. My wife Lucy doesn't like potatoes but she likes mushrooms. For meat, I like chicken and my wife also likes chicken. I like tea but my wife likes coffee.

I have two children, Erica and David. Erica doesn't like pizza but she likes pasta. David loves pizza but doesn't like pasta. For vegetables, Erica likes everything. David likes most things but he doesn't like broccoli. Erica doesn't like tea or coffee but David likes tea sometimes.

1) Does the writer like carrots?

2) What vegetables does the writer like?

3) Does the writer like mushrooms?

4) What do the writer and his wife both like?

5) Who likes tea?

6) Does David like pasta?

7) What doesn't David like?

8) Does Erica like coffee?

Extension – Write at least 5 more questions about the text:

Do you like...?

Do you like _____ ? ⟶ Yes, I do.
⟶ No, I don't.

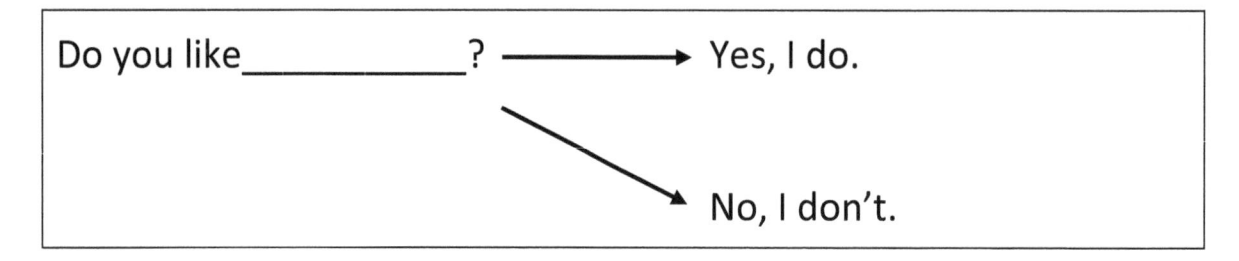

Ask your partner these questions and **circle** *their answers:*

Do you like…

cooking?	Yes, I do.	No, I don't.
shopping?	Yes, I do.	No, I don't.
learning English?	Yes, I do.	No, I don't.
travelling?	Yes, I do.	No, I don't.
the UK?	Yes, I do.	No, I don't.
your home?	Yes, I do.	No, I don't.
your family?	Yes, I do.	No, I don't.
your town?	Yes, I do.	No, I don't.
watching TV?	Yes, I do.	No, I don't.
doing exercise?	Yes, I do.	No, I don't.
animals?	Yes, I do.	No, I don't.
playing games?	Yes, I do.	No, I don't.
drinking alcohol?	Yes, I do.	No, I don't.
dancing?	Yes, I do.	No, I don't.

Extension – make more questions to ask your partner:

Writing Practice

*Write 10 things that you **like**:*

1) I like………

2) ……

3) ……

4) ……

5) ……

6) ……

7) ……

8) ……

9) ……

10) ………

*Write 10 things that you **don't like**:*

1) I don't like………………………………………………………………………………………………………

2) ……

3) ……

4) ……

5) ……

6) ……

7) ……

8) ……

9) ……

10) ………

Like/Don't Like Speaking Practice

1) you/like/do/learning/English?

2) what/you/do/like/food?

3) drink/you/what/do/like?

4) do/you/where/best/country/this/in/like?

5) best/where/you/do/like/your/in/country?

6) you/like/singing/dancing/and/do?

7) sports/what/you/like/do?

8) you/like/do/your/home?

9) like/you/do/town/your?

10) TV/programmes/you/do/like/what?

11) like/music/what/do/you?

12) you/like/why/do/your/friends?

13) you/like/cats/dogs/do/or?

14) what/transport/you/do/like?

Extension – make at least 5 more questions to ask your partner:

Common Mistakes – Like/Don't like

Find the mistakes in these sentences and write the correct version below:

1) I am like my friend.

....

2) Steve is no like his house.

....

3) We is like cat and dog.

....

4) Are you like cooking?

....

5) She is no like go to the gym.

....

6) What do you like food?

....

7) Is he likes go to the park?

....

8) Peter and John likes eating food.

....

9) We are no like the new restaurant.

....

10) My friend he like going shopping.

....

11) What do he like colour?

....

12) Why you no like meet me for a coffee?

....

Present Simple Tense

FORM:
I/You/We/They **play**; He/She/It **plays**

NEGATIVE FORM:
I/You/We/They **don't** play; He/she/It **doesn't** play

Use for: Habits/routines

Change the verbs into to the correct form and put in the gaps:

1) Bill _____ playing football (like).

2) Sally _____ shopping every day (go).

3) They _____ TV every night (watch).

4) Adam and Mia _____ the bus every weekday (take).

5) Erika _____ anymore because she is too busy (swim).

6) She _____ a cup of tea every afternoon (drink).

7) Al and Ed _____ tennis every weekend (play).

8) My college _____ at 9 o'clock (start).

9) I _____ college at about 4 o'clock (leave).

10) What a nice dress, mum. You _____ beautiful (look).

11) Fred _____ anymore because he has a bad back (run).

12) Mel _____ very hard in her job (work).

13) Mary _____ dinner for her family every night (cook).

14) Bob and Suzi _____ each other very much (love).

15) We _____ our parents every night (call).

16) I _____ a car anymore (drive).

Derek's Day

Derek wakes up at 7am. He goes downstairs and eats his breakfast. He eats toast with a little butter. He drinks a cup of tea. At 7:30 he takes a shower and brushes his teeth. Then he gets dressed.

He leaves his house at 8am and goes to the bus stop. He takes the bus for 20 minutes to his college. His lesson starts at 9:30. He studies English. Lunchbreak is at 12:30. His break is 1 hour. He eats a sandwich and he drinks a cup of tea. His lesson finishes at 4pm. He takes the bus home and arrives home at 4:30.

At home he relaxes for 1 hour. Then he cooks dinner. He cooks rice or pasta and meat. He eats about 6:30. After dinner he watches TV for about 1 hour.

He goes to bed at 10. He reads a book for 1 hour then goes to sleep.

1) What time does he wake up?

2) What does he eat for breakfast?

3) What time does he brush his teeth?

4) How long does he take the bus?

5) What time does his college start?

6) What time does he arrive home?

7) What does he cook?

8) What time does he sleep?

Extension – make at least 5 more questions about the text:

Present Simple Speaking Practice

1) what/you/do/do/Saturdays/on?

2) do/what/do/you/on/Sundays?

3) time/do/you/up/get/what/morning/every?

4) usually/what/you/breakfast/eat/do/for?

5) time/what/you/do/leave/house/your?

6) often/how/bus/take/a/you/do?

7) eat/for/you/do/what/lunch?

8) go/shopping/when/do/you?

9) what/eat/you/usually/dinner/for/do?

10) watch/TV/when/you/do?

11) usually/drink/what/you/do?

12) you/relax/how/do?

13) often/how/you/do/your/house/clean?

14) time/what/you/do/bed/to/go?

Extension – mark at least 5 more questions to ask your partner:

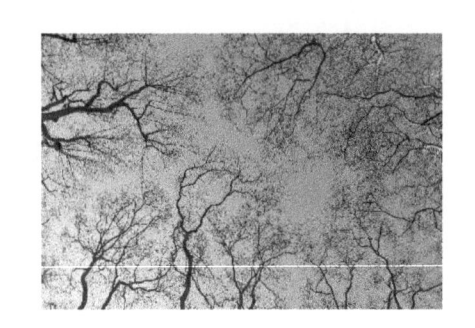

Danny's Day

Danny wakes up at 6:30 every morning. First he goes downstairs and eats breakfast. He eats a slice of toast and drinks a cup of tea with milk. After breakfast he takes a shower at about 7am. Then he brushes his teeth and gets dressed. He leaves his house at 8am. He takes the train to work. He gets to work at 8:45. He starts work at 9am.

His lunch break is at 12:30 for 1 hour. He eats lunch with his colleagues. He usually has a sandwich and a cup of coffee. After lunch he goes back to work. He finishes work at 5pm. Then he takes the train home.

He gets home at 6pm. At home he rests for 30 minutes then cooks dinner. After dinner he watches TV for an hour. He goes to bed at 10:30 and reads a book in bed for an hour then goes to sleep.

1) What time does Danny wake up?

2) What does he eat for breakfast?

3) What time does he take a shower?

4) How does he go to work?

5) What time does he start work?

6) What time does he start work after his lunch break?

7) What time does he get home?

8) What time does he cook dinner?

9) What does he do after dinner?

10) What time does he sleep?

Extension – write at least 5 more questions about the text:

Writing Practice

*Write 10 things that you **do every day**:*

1) I ....

2) ....

3) ....

4) ....

5) ....

6) ....

7) ....

8) ....

9) ....

10) ....

*Write 10 things that you **don't do every day**:*

1) I don't ....

2) ....

3) ....

4) ....

5) ....

6) ....

7) ....

8) ....

9) ....

10) ....

Present Simple Crossword

ACROSS
2. He doesn't _____ fish.
5. I _____ TV at night.
6. I _____ football every day.
8. I _____ a lot of tea.
12. Mike _____ every night.
13. He _____ early every night.
14. I _____ at home at weekends.
15. She _____ a bus to college.
16. Ben _____ to school.

DOWN
1. I _____ my clothes at home.
3. Max _____ with his dad every day.
4. I _____ my food in the shop.
5. She _____ up at 8am.
7. Do you _____ to church?
9. He _____ in the park.
10. Adam _____ his room often.
11. He _____ his friend often.
12. She _____ her mum daily.

Present Simple Mistakes

Find the mistakes in these sentences and write the correct version below:

1) I am go to the park every day.

....

2) Sarah watch TV every night.

....

3) They studies English at the college.

....

4) Are you brush your teeth every day?

....

5) He is not swim in the pool every summer.

....

6) My friend he visit me every evening.

....

7) What time you do get up in the morning usually?

....

8) He listen to the radio at home.

....

9) What time do the shop open?

....

10) I am like my job very much.

....

11) Does he likes playing football?

....

12) My cat it play in the garden at night.

....

Present Continuous

> FORM: I **am** (not); You/We/They **are** (not) + **Verb + ing**
> He/She/It **is** (not) + **Verb + ing**
> 1) Actions happening now
> 2) Future arrangements (know time & place)

Put the correct form of present continuous in the gaps (some are negative):

1) Adam _____ because he is so tired (sleep).

2) We _____ TV because there is a football match on (watch).

3) The man _____ because he is happy (laugh).

4) Lucy _____ as a cleaner in an office at the moment (work).

5) What _____ you _____ now (do)?

6) We _____ our friend in the park this afternoon (meet).

7) Ben and Lily _____ in Scotland at the moment (live).

8) I _____ any beer tonight because I have a bad stomach (drink).

9) When _____ you _____ on holiday this year (go)?

10) Ben _____ today because he is very sick (work).

11) Phil _____ in the race next week (run).

12) I'm sad because the sun _____ (shine).

13) It _____ very heavily outside (rain).

14) I can't call you because my phone _____ anymore (work).

15) The grass in my garden _____ quickly after the rains (grow).

16) The doorbell _____. I need to answer it (ring).

17) We _____ in the park because it's raining (run).

18) Norman _____ tennis next week (play).

Present Continuous Speaking Practice

1) you/are/what/now/doing?

2) going/where/the/you/are/weekend/at?

3) studying/where/you/are/now?

4) the/who/meeting/after/are/you/lesson?

5) at/friend/the/what/doing/moment/is/your?

6) going/next/trip/where/are/your/you/for?

7) friend/where/living/now/your/is?

8) eating/what/drinking/are/and/you/tonight?

9) moment/studying/anything/you/at/the/are?

10) you/are/watching/tonight/TV?

11) raining/tomorrow/is/it?

12) you/are/your/enjoying/lessons/English?

Extension – write at least 5 more questions to ask your partner:

1) ....

2) ....

3) ....

4) ....

5) ....

Writing Practice

*Write 8 **positive** sentences using **present continuous**:*

1) ....

2) ....

3) ....

4) ....

5) ....

6) ....

7) ....

8) ....

*Write 8 **negative** sentences using **present continuous**:*

1) ....

2) ....

3) ....

4) ....

5) ....

6) ....

7) ....

8) ....

Present Continuous Crossword

ACROSS
4. I _____ juice now.
5. They _____ a letter.
8. I _____ to good music.
10. She _____ a beautiful dress.
11. The nice man _____ at me.
13. They _____ football.
14. My flowers _____ very tall.
15. I _____ on a bus now.
17. She _____ a train.

DOWN
1. I _____ a good book.
2. He _____ in the park.
3. The children _____ a nice song.
6. We _____ TV now.
7. The bird _____ in the sky.
9. I _____ to the supermarket.
10. My dad _____ a nice meal.
12. It _____ a lot outside.
16. She _____ fish at the moment.

Mistakes – Present Continuous

Find the mistakes in these sentences and write the correct version below:

1) John and Jill is swimming in the sea.

....

2) Mike is no reading a book at the moment.

....

3) They is watching TV in the living room.

....

4) They is runing in the park.

....

5) I no am study English now.

....

6) She is call her friend now?

....

7) Adam he is write a letter now.

....

8) Ann is relax on the sofa now.

....

9) She is learn English at school now.

....

10) You are speaking to me?

....

11) I can't talk because I am work now.

....

12) She no is cook dinner now.

....

Past Tense (Regular)

For the past just add "-ed"

Clean > clean**ed**

Watch > watch**ed**

Play > play**ed**

BUT: *Usually* "**Y**" *changes to* "**i**" *when you add* "**-ed**"

Copy > cop**ied**   Study > stud**ied**

*Change these words to the **past** then put them in the spaces:*

relax/visit/cook/clean/wash/start/copy/study/play/call/help/watch

1) Steve and Adam _____ football in the park yesterday.

2) We _____ a good film on TV last night.

3) She _____ a nice meal for her friend.

4) I _____ my friend's house in the morning.

5) We _____ our clothes in the washing machine.

6) He _____ at home on his sofa at the weekend.

7) I _____ my flat last weekend.

8) They _____ English at college yesterday.

9) Mary _____ a beautiful picture from a book.

10) The lesson _____ at 9:30 am but Aris and Odahir were late.

11) I _____ my friend clean her house.

12) I _____ my parents on the phone last night.

Past Regular: Negative and Questions

Positive	Negative	Question
He clean**ed**	He **didn't** clean	**Did** he clean?
I watch**ed**	I **didn't** watch	**Did** you watch?
We play**ed**	We **didn't** play	**Did** we play?

*Change these words to the **past** then put them in the correct form in the gaps below (some are negative):*

watch/enjoy/cook/dance/relax/jump/clean/smile/call/work/visit/stay

1) My friend _____ an Italian meal for me.

2) We _____ the delicious dinner my mother cooked.

3) _____ you _____ your friend on the phone last night?

4) Susan _____ at the café yesterday because she had a cold.

5) We _____ at the party for a long time last night.

6) My family _____ a good film on TV last night.

7) I didn't go out at the weekend, I just _____ at home.

8) Carmen _____ her relatives because she was sick.

9) The man _____ because he was very happy.

10) I _____ my flat because I was too busy.

11) My friend _____ on the sofa because he was tired.

12) _____ your cat _____ onto the roof?

Writing Practice

*Write 8 **positive** sentences using the **regular past**:*

1) ....

2) ....

3) ....

4) ....

5) ....

6) ....

7) ....

8) ....

*Write 8 **negative** sentences using the **regular past**:*

1) ....

2) ....

3) ....

4) ....

5) ....

6) ....

7) ....

8) ....

Did/Didn't

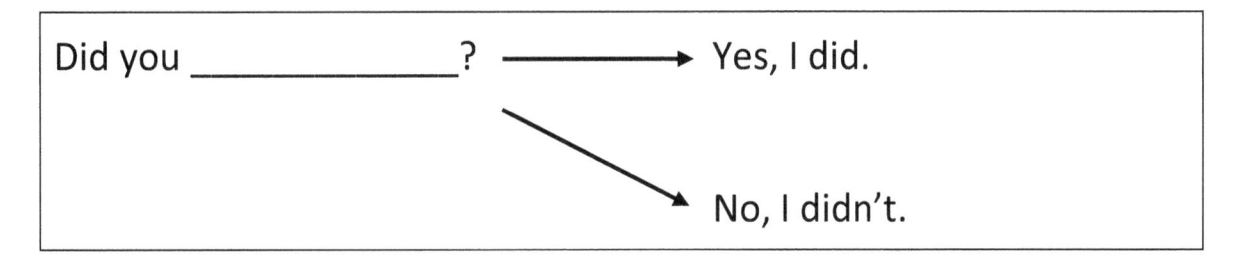

Did you _____ ? ⟶ Yes, I did.

⟶ No, I didn't.

Ask your partner these questions and **circle** their answers:

Did you …

study yesterday?	Yes, I did.	No, I didn't.
climb a tree yesterday?	Yes, I did.	No, I didn't.
cook last night?	Yes, I did.	No, I didn't.
smile yesterday?	Yes, I did.	No, I didn't.
watch TV last night?	Yes, I did.	No, I didn't.
play football last week?	Yes, I did.	No, I didn't.
walk last weekend?	Yes, I did.	No, I didn't.
play a game last week?	Yes, I did.	No, I didn't.
wash yesterday?	Yes, I did.	No, I didn't.
clean your home yesterday?	Yes, I did.	No, I didn't.
travel last year?	Yes, I did.	No, I didn't.
relax last night?	Yes, I did.	No, I didn't.
call your friend yesterday?	Yes, I did.	No, I didn't.
help anyone last week?	Yes, I did.	No, I didn't.

Writing Practice

*Write questions with **did** to ask your partner:*

1) Did you ……………………………………………………………………………………………………

2) ………

3) ………

4) ………

5) ………

6) ………

7) ………

8) ………

9) ………

10) ……

11) ……

12) ……

13) ……

14) ……

15) ……

Dahira's Dinner

Mary called her friend Dahira on Friday and visited her in her flat last weekend. Dahira cooked dinner. She cooked roast chicken and potatoes. Mary liked the chicken but she didn't like the potatoes. They talked for a long time at the dinner table. They talked about work and their boyfriends. Both of them cleaned the dirty dishes and glasses in the sink.

After the meal Mary and Dahira listened to pop music. Dahira danced but Mary didn't. Then they relaxed on the sofa and watched TV. They watched a Japanese film. Mary stayed for four hours at Dahira's home. They both enjoyed the evening very much.

1) Underline all the past tense verbs in the text. How many are there?

2) How many sentences are there?

3) What did Dahira cook?

4) Did Mary like the potatoes?

5) What did they talk about?

6) What did they clean?

7) Did Mary dance?

8) What music did they listen to?

9) How long did Mary stay there?

10) Did they enjoy the evening?

Extension – make at least 5 more questions about the text:

Past Regular Speaking Practice

1) who/last/call/you/did/week?

2) visit/who/did/you/weekend/last?

3) travel/year/where/last/did/you?

4) when/home/clean/you/did/your?

5) you/study/what/did/your/in/lesson?

6) where/walk/you/did/last/week?

7) you/did/play/game/last/week/a?

8) cook/what/you/did/weekend/at/the?

9) you/did/to/listen/music/week/last?

10) watch/what/TV/on/did/you?

11) you/did/enjoy/weekend/your?

12) yesterday/how/you/did/relax?

Extension – make at least 5 more questions in the past to ask your partner:

Common Mistakes – Past Tense Regular

Find the mistakes in these sentences and write the correct version below:

1) He was played football in the park.

   ....

2) Did he watched a film on TV?

   ....

3) My friend no did visit me last weekend.

   ....

4) Bill he was listen to music yesterday.

   ....

5) I cook a delicious meal for my family.

   ....

6) We studyed very hard at college.

   ....

7) Adam didn't relaxed at home because he was busy.

   ....

8) You did call your brother yesterday?

   ....

9) What time the lesson started.

   ....

10) Are you washed your clothes?

    ....

11) My friend is called me last night.

    ....

12) I am cleaned my house because it was dirty.

    ....

"Be" Verb Past: Positive

Copy the past "be" verb into the box

I was	
You were	
He was	
She was	
It was	
We were	
They were	

Write the correct form of the "be" verb:

1) The food _____ delicious.

2) I _____ in Spain last year.

3) They _____ happy.

4) You _____ very tired.

5) He _____ a kind man.

6) We _____ very happy.

7) My class _____ fun.

8) I _____ sick yesterday.

9) The weather _____ cold.

10) Irene and Lama _____ tired.

11) Nicola _____ early.

12) She _____ a teacher.

13) My clothes _____ new.

14) I _____ hungry.

15) The meal _____ cheap.

16) It _____ sunny today.

17) They _____ very late.

18) The food _____ spicy.

19) Eliza _____ slim.

20) The restaurant _____ very busy.

Writing Practice

*Write 8 sentences using **was**:*

1) ....

2) ....

3) ....

4) ....

5) ....

6) ....

7) ....

8) ....

*Write 8 sentences using **were**:*

1) ....

2) ....

3) ....

4) ....

5) ....

6) ....

7) ....

8) ....

"Be" Verb Past - Negative

Copy the past "be" verb into the box

I was not	
You were not	
He was not	
She was not	
It was not	
We were not	
They were not	

Write the correct negative form of the "be" verb:

1) He _____ angry with me.

2) They _____ rich.

3) The food _____ expensive.

4) The restaurant _____ clean.

5) His car _____ old.

6) I _____ late for college.

7) It _____ a nice day.

8) Mike _____ tired.

9) My friend _____ cold.

10) The women _____ nice.

11) He _____ a cleaner.

12) The weather _____ hot.

13) I _____ sad today.

14) She _____ very kind.

15) Her trousers _____ new.

16) My friends _____ there.

17) They _____ clever.

18) You _____ slow.

19) The street _____ long.

20) Aris and Dora _____ on time for the lesson.

Writing Practice

*Write 8 sentences using **was not**:*

1) ....

2) ....

3) ....

4) ....

5) ....

6) ....

7) ....

8) ....

*Write 8 sentences using **were not**:*

1) ....

2) ....

3) ....

4) ....

5) ....

6) ....

7) ....

8) ....

Was/Were Speaking Practice

1) was/how/weather/yesterday/the?

2) last/where/you/were/week?

3) home/last/were/you/at/weekend?

4) was/what/dinner/your/yesterday?

5) your/who/was/teacher/school/at?

6) you/were/good/at/school/a/student?

7) you/were/late/your/lesson/English/for/week/last?

8) happy/last/sad/or/you/were/week?

9) long/were/you/how/in/last/your/home?

10) was/where/your/trip/last?

11) memory/last/happiest/was/year/what/from/your?

12) were/friends'/country/in/your/what/your/names?

Extension – make at least 5 more questions to ask your partner:

1)………

2)………

3)………

4)………

5)………

Common Mistakes – Was/Were

Find the mistakes in these sentences and write the correct version below:

1) We no was happy yesterday.

....

2) Where you was yesterday?

....

3) She was no in the gym when I went.

....

4) What were your favourite food as a child?

....

5) Why you wasn't at school yesterday.

....

6) My trousers was clean.

....

7) You were in the library yesterday?

....

8) I were sad that I couldn't see you.

....

9) I am sorry I were late for college yesterday.

....

10) Who were he with last week?

....

11) We was very tired after the lesson.

....

12) Was Peter and John happy at the party?

....

Past Irregular

Match the verbs with their past tense:

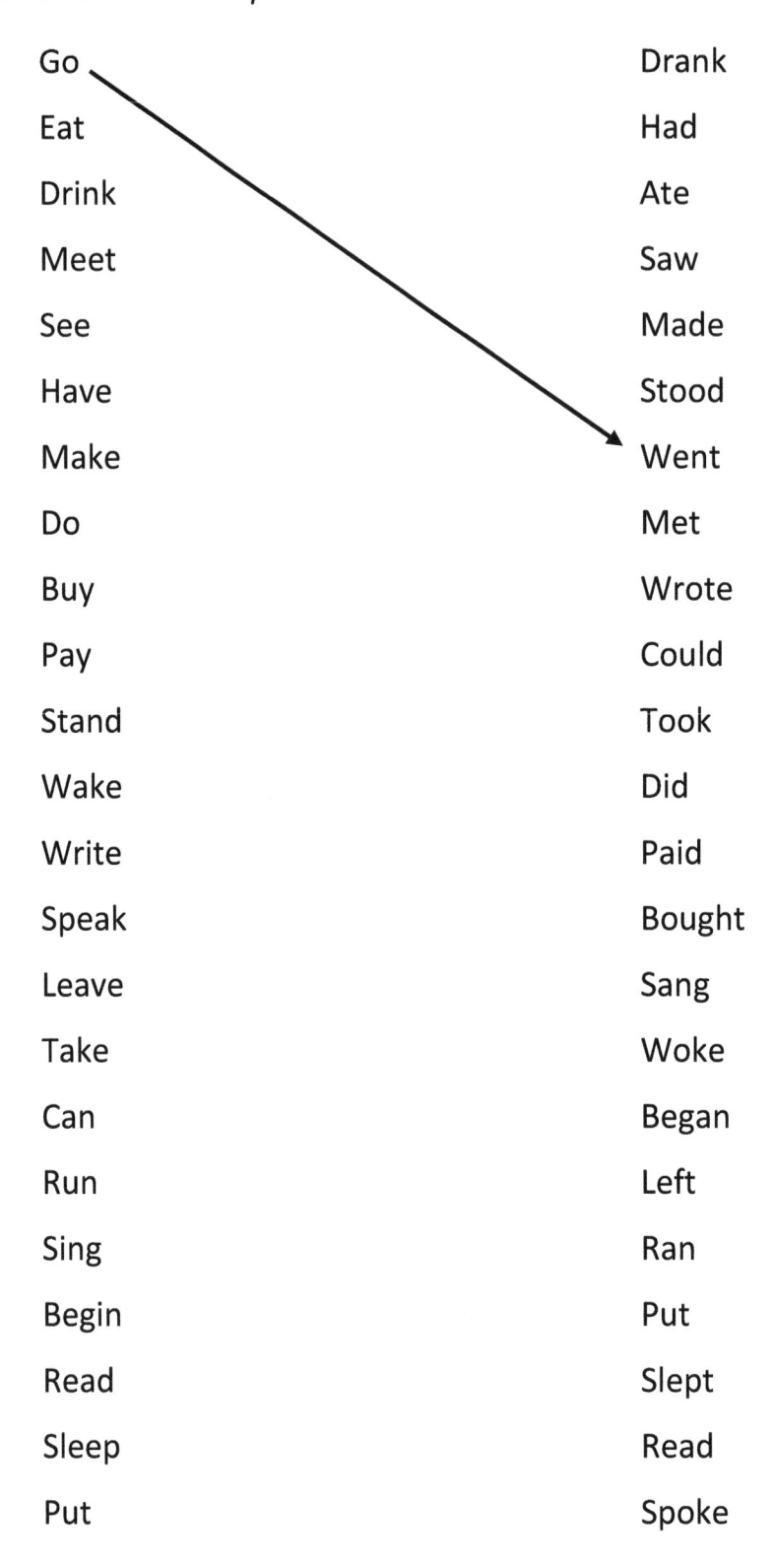

Go	Drank
Eat	Had
Drink	Ate
Meet	Saw
See	Made
Have	Stood
Make	Went
Do	Met
Buy	Wrote
Pay	Could
Stand	Took
Wake	Did
Write	Paid
Speak	Bought
Leave	Sang
Take	Woke
Can	Began
Run	Left
Sing	Ran
Begin	Put
Read	Slept
Sleep	Read
Put	Spoke

Past Tense Irregular

Fill in the past of these verbs:

Verb	Past	Verb	Past	Verb	Past	Verb	Past
Begin		Go		Meet		Sleep	
Buy		Have		Pay		Speak	
Can		Is		Read		Stand	
Do		Know		Run		Take	
Drink		Leave		See		Wake	
Eat		Make		Sing		Write	

*First change these words to the **past** then put them in the spaces:*

speak/buy/sleep/write/do/drink/pay/meet/see/have/take/eat/run/go

1) Adam _____ his homework yesterday.

2) We _____ very well last night because we were tired.

3) He _____ a text message to his girlfriend.

4) I _____ to my friend on the phone last night.

5) They _____ a nice meal in a restaurant.

6) Peter _____ a glass of orange juice because he was thirsty.

7) Tim _____ some food in the supermarket.

8) I _____ my friends in the park at the weekend.

9) When I was in the street, I _____ a big dog.

10) I _____ the bus to work last week.

11) Norman _____ no time to meet me.

12) We _____ a lot of money to go to the gym.

13) They _____ on holiday to Spain last year.

14) Last summer I _____ in the park every morning.

Writing Practice

*Write 8 positive sentences using the **irregular past**:*

1) ....

2) ....

3) ....

4) ....

5) ....

6) ....

7) ....

8) ....

*Write 8 negative sentences using the **irregular past**:*

1) ....

2) ....

3) ....

4) ....

5) ....

6) ....

7) ....

8) ....

William's Weekend

Last weekend William took the train to Bristol to meet his friend Gary. He met his friend Saturday at 1pm at the station. They went to the park together for a picnic. After lunch they played football and then walked by the river. In the evening they went to a restaurant. William ate chicken and Gary ate beef. They both drank beer. Gary paid the bill and they went home and saw a film.

On Sunday they woke up at 8am and ran in the park for an hour. They came home and took a shower. They went shopping. Gary bought food for lunch. After lunch they said goodbye and William took the train home.

1) Underline all the past tense verbs in the text. How many are there?

2) How many sentences are there?

3) Where did William go?

4) What time did they meet?

5) What did they eat in the restaurant?

6) What did they do at home?

7) What time did they wake up?

8) How long did they run in the park?

9) What did Gary buy?

10) Where did William go after lunch?

Extension – make at least 5 more questions about the text:

Past Irregular Speaking Practice

1) what/last/do/you/did/week?

2) meet/who/did/weekend/you/last?

3) go/year/where/last/did/you?

4) eat/what/drink/did/you/and/night/last?

5) job/what/did/you/your/do/in/country?

6) where/you/live/a/did/as/child?

7) bus/last/when/you/did/take/a?

8) where/best/place/is/went/last/year/the/you?

9) what/did/you/read/book/last?

10) when/last/sing/dance/or/you/did?

11) buy/week/what/did/you/last?

12) what/you/wake/up/did/time/morning/this?

Extension – make at least 5 more questions in the past to ask your partner:

Past Crossword

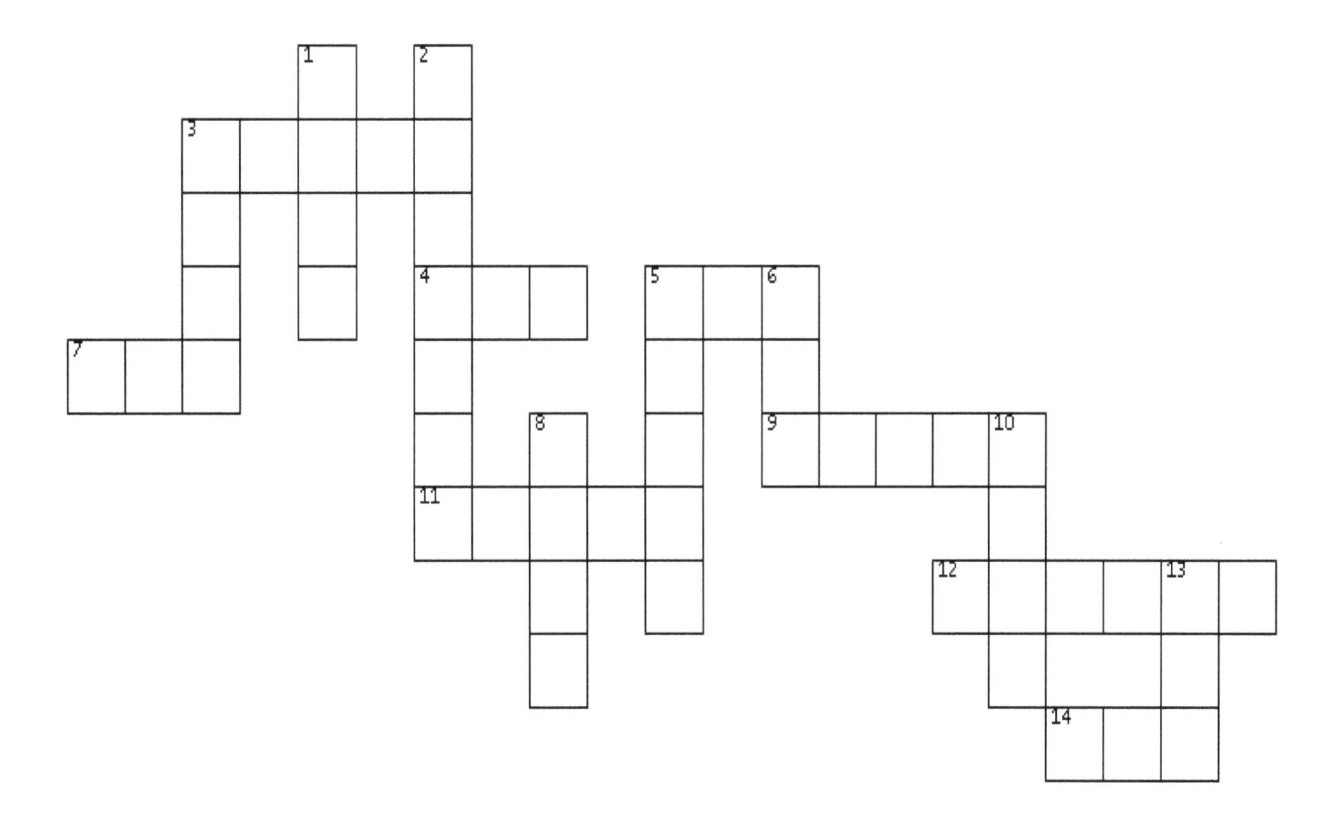

ACROSS
3. I _____ a text message.
4. Ben _____ a cake.
5. He _____ me running for the bus.
7. Sam _____ his friend yesterday.
9. He _____ late last night.
11. Ed _____ some coffee.
12. She _____ a new car.
14. She _____ her homework.

DOWN
1. He _____ up late.
2. He _____ on his sofa.
3. I _____ to the park last week.
5. I _____ to my mother
6. I _____ sick yesterday.
8. He _____ to class late.
10. She _____ the bus yesterday.
13. Sue _____ a headache.

Common Mistakes – Past Tense Irregular

Find the mistakes in these sentences and write the correct version below:

1) I did read a book last night.

....

2) Tom did go to the gym yesterday?

....

3) He was take the train to his office.

....

4) Did you met your friend in the supermarket?

....

5) Peter eated delicious food yesterday.

....

6) Susan no drunk coffee in the café.

....

7) We leaved the college very late last night.

....

8) Mike was read a book at school.

....

9) She buyed some broccoli from the shop.

....

10) Did you spoke with your parents yesterday?

....

11) Mary didn't waked up very early this morning.

....

12) I can play the piano when I was five years old.

....

Question Forms

For **present/past simple tenses** (not "*be*" verb):

Question word	Auxiliary verb	Person/thing	infinitive	...
Where	Do	you	live?	
How many pens	does	he	have?	
	Does	she	like	dogs?
What	did	you	do	yesterday?
Where	did	he	eat?	

For **present/past simple tenses** for "*be*" verb:

Question word	"be"	Person/thing	...
How	are	you?	
	Is	he	nice?
What	is	your	name?
Where	was	the pen?	
Who	were	they?	

Ask these questions to Bill:

1) (Where/from) "_____?" "Britain."

2) (Where/live now) "_____?" "In Oxford."

3) (What/your hobby) "_____?" "Chess."

4) (How often/play) "_____?" "Every day."

5) (Married) "_____?" "Yes, I am."

6) (Children) "_____?" "Yes, I do."

7) (How old/they) "_____?" "6 and 8."

8) (What/wife do) "_____?" "She's a chef."

9) (She/like her job) "_____?" "Yes, she does."

10) (How often/work) "_____?" "She works 5 days/week."

Speaking Practice

Make questions with these prompts then ask your partner:

1) Where/you/live? _____

2) Do/like/your area? _____

3) Where/live/before? _____

4) When/born? _____

5) Where/born? _____

6) What/do? _____

7) How/get/to college? _____

8) Married? _____

9) Children? _____

10) How many brothers/sisters? _____

11) Who/like best in your family? _____

12) Who/best friend? _____

13) What/hobby? _____

14) How often/exercise? _____

15) What/do/last weekend? _____

16) Who/meet/last weekend? _____

Extension – make at least 5 more questions to ask your partner:

Future Plans – "going to"

Fill in the gaps below:

Positive +	Negative -	Question ?
I am going to…	I am not going to…	Am I going to…?
You		
He		
She		
It		
We		
They		

cook/run/watch/visit/drink/go/clean/play/buy/stay/call/go

Put the verbs into the spaces:

1) I'm going to _____ TV at home tonight.

2) My friend is going to _____ a nice dinner for me.

3) We are going to _____ food in the supermarket.

4) She's going to _____ in the local park tomorrow.

5) We're going to _____ at home all day.

6) Dora is going to _____ football with her friends.

7) I'm going to _____ my best friend tonight.

8) He's going to _____ his room.

9) I'm going to _____ my mum on the phone.

10) She's going to _____ coffee in the café now.

11) We are going to _____ to the gym.

12) We are going to _____ shopping after class.

Going to: Short Answers

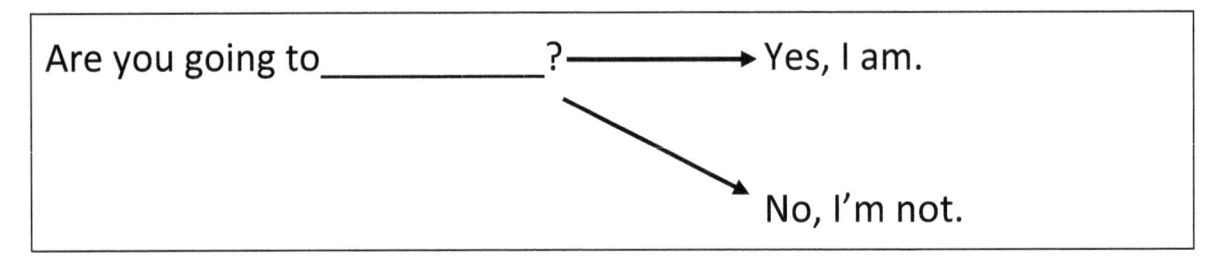

Are you going to _____? → Yes, I am.
 → No, I'm not.

Ask your partner these questions and **circle** their answers:

Are you going to…

cook tonight?	Yes, I am.	No, I'm not.
go shopping tomorrow?	Yes, I am.	No, I'm not.
learn English tonight?	Yes, I am.	No, I'm not.
watch TV tonight?	Yes, I am.	No, I'm not.
call a friend tonight?	Yes, I am.	No, I'm not.
listen to music today?	Yes, I am.	No, I'm not.
run at the weekend?	Yes, I am.	No, I'm not.
see your family tonight?	Yes, I am.	No, I'm not.
travel next year?	Yes, I am.	No, I'm not.
exercise at the weekend?	Yes, I am.	No, I'm not.
dance tomorrow?	Yes, I am.	No, I'm not.
play a game tomorrow?	Yes, I am.	No, I'm not.
work at the weekend?	Yes, I am.	No, I'm not.
drink coffee later?	Yes, I am.	No, I'm not.

Extension – make more questions to ask your partner:

William's Weekend Work

William is a waiter. He works in a restaurant in Cardiff. He is going to start work on Saturday night at 5pm. He is going to prepare the tables first. He is going to work for 7 hours. He is going to finish at 12am. Then he is going to go home by bus.

On Sunday he is going to start at 11am. He is going to serve lunch. He is going to have a break at 3pm. He is going to finish at 6pm. Then he is going to take the bus home. His job is very hard but he likes it very much.

Answer these questions about the text using full sentences:

1) What is William's job?

2) Where does he work?

3) What time is he going to start work on Saturday?

4) What is he going to do first on Saturday?

5) How long is he going to work on Saturday night?

6) What time is he going to work on Sunday?

7) What is he going to do at the restaurant on Sunday?

8) How long is he going to work on Sunday?

9) What time is he going to finish on Sunday?

10) How is he going to go home?

Extension – make at least 3 more questions about the text:

1) ....

2) ....

3) ....

Writing Practice

*Write 10 positive sentences using **going to**:*

1) ....

2) ....

3) ....

4) ....

5) ....

6) ....

7) ....

8) ....

9) ....

10) ....

*Write 10 negative sentences using **going to**:*

1) ....

2) ....

3) ....

4) ....

5) ....

6) ....

7) ....

8) ....

9) ....

10) ....

Going to Speaking Practice

1) do/what/going/you/are/to/the/after/lesson?

2) tonight/going/what/do/you/are/to?

3) weekend/what/you/at/going/do/are/the/to?

4) dinner/what/going/eat/are/drink/and/you/to/for?

5) what/going/you/are/to/to/go/time/tonight/bed?

6) you/out/time/what/tomorrow/bed/of/get/are/going/to?

7) next/what/do/going/you/are/year/to?

8) shopping/next/when/you/are/going/go/to?

9) which/friend/you/are/meet/next/to/going?

10) weekend/wear/going/what/at/the/you/are/to?

11) live/you/going/future/in/where/are/to/the?

12) job/you/what/do/future/the/in/going/to/are?

Extension – make at least 5 more questions to ask your partner:

1) ……………………………………………………………………………………………

2) ……………………………………………………………………………………………

3) ……………………………………………………………………………………………

4) ……………………………………………………………………………………………

5) ……………………………………………………………………………………………

Going to Crossword

ACROSS
2. She is going to _____ her mum.
4. He isn't going to _____ English.
5. I'm not going to _____ a film.
8. He isn't going to _____ a car.
9. I am going to _____ dinner.
11. We are going to _____ TV.
12. Adam is going to _____ in the park.
14. She is going to _____ rice.

DOWN
1. Tom is going to _____ football.
3. I am going to _____ a book.
4. We aren't going to _____ early.
5. The lesson is going to _____ at 9:30.
6. He is going to _____ his friend.
7. I am going to _____ my house.
10. I am going to _____ tea.
13. They aren't going to _____ shopping.

Common Mistakes – Going to

Find the mistakes in these sentences and write the correct version below:

1) You is going to meet your friend?

....

2) They is going to watching TV tonight.

....

3) I is going to drink a cup of tea.

....

4) Sarah she is no going to read a book.

....

5) They is going to eating in a restaurant.

....

6) Michael is no going to climb a mountain at the weekend.

....

7) You are going to play football?

....

8) Lisa is go to take a bus to go to work.

....

9) I am sad because my friend going to living in the USA.

....

10) Mary going to play tennis with his friend.

....

11) I going to call my friend tonight.

....

12) You are going work tomorrow?

....

Answer key

Be Verb Positive

1) are 2) are 3) is 4) are 5) is 6) am 7) is 8) am 9) is 10) are 11) am 12) is 13) is 14) is 15) is 16) is 17) am 18) is 19) are 20) are

Be Verb Negative

1) are not 2) are not 3) is not 4) is not 5) is not 6) am not 7) is not 8) is not 9) is not 10) are not 11) is not 12) is not 13) am not 14) am not 15) am not 16) are not 17) are not 18) are not 19) are not 20) is not

My Friend

1) He is 35 years old. 2) He is a waiter. 3) His hobby is swimming. 4) Yes, he is. 5) Her name is Mary. 6) No, she isn't. 7) She is a childminder. 8) Their names are Ana and Maria. 9) Ana is 7 and Maria is 10 years old. 10) They are pupils at a school in their town.

Be Verb Speaking Practice

1) What is your name? 2) Are you happy today? 3) What is your hobby? 4) Are you married? 5) What is your address? 6) What is your job? 7) How is the weather today? 8) Are you hungry now? 9) What is your favourite food? 10) What is your favourite drink? 11) What is your country's name? 12) Who is your best friend? 13) What are your friends' names? 14) Where are your friends now?

Common Mistakes: Be Verb

1) I am not happy. 2) John is a nice man. 3) Are you busy today? 4) I am a very lucky woman. 5) My favourite food is pizza. 6) Is my teacher sick today? 7) I am not late because I took the bus. 8) Simon is very hungry. 9) I am not tired today. 10) They are my friends. 11) Tom and Sarah are nice people. 12) We are always nice to people.

Have /Has Positive

1) has 2) have 3) have 4) have 5) have 6) have 7) have 8) has 9) has 10) have 11) has 12) have 13) has 14) has 15) has 16) has 17) have 18) has 19) has 20) has

Have/has Negative

1) doesn't have 2) don't have 3) doesn't have 4) don't have 5) don't have 6) doesn't have 7) don't have 8) don't have 9) doesn't have 10) don't have 11) don't have 12) doesn't have 13) doesn't have 14) doesn't have 15) doesn't have 16) don't have 17) don't have 18) doesn't have 19) doesn't have 20) doesn't have

Common Mistakes: Have

1) He has a nice car. 2) We don't have time to meet you today. 3) Do you have the time? 4) She has long, black hair. 5) Ben and Billy have new books. 6) I have a nice teacher. 7) I don't have much money in my pocket. 8) William has a big house. 9) You don't have new shoes. 10) We have a party at my house tomorrow. 11) My mother has very nice friends. 12) Ron doesn't have a brother.

Possessives

1) my 2) her 3) your 4) our 5) their 6) her 7) its 8) his 9) her 10) her 11) my 12) her

Can/can't

1) can 2) can't 3) can 4) can't 5) can 6) Can 7) can't 8) can 9) can 10) can 11) can't 12) Can 13) can't 14) can't 15) Can 16) can't 17) can 18) can

Can/can't Reading: The Smith Family

1) There are 4 people in the Smith family. 2) John can. 3) John can't. 4) She can cook pasta, fish and meat. 5) He is good at art. 6) Yes, he can. 7) He can't play a musical instrument. 8) She can play 3 instruments. 9) She can sing very well. 10) Yes, she can.

Can/Can't Speaking Practice

1) Can you drive a car? 2) Can you ride a bicycle? 3) What can you cook best? 4) Can you play chess? 5) Can you swim well? 6) What sport can you do best? 7) Can you play a musical instrument? 8) What languages can you speak? 9) How far can you run? 10) How long can you sleep? 11) Can you paint or draw a picture? 12) How can you practise your English? 13) Can you sing or dance well? 14) What can you see from your window in your home?

Common Mistakes: Can/Can't

1) We can run in the park. 2) Linda can't dance. 3) Can you help my friend? 4) She can play the piano. 5) He can drive a car. 6) I can't understand you. 7) She can sing and dance beautifully. 8) Can you use a computer? 9) I can't come to class today because I am sick. 10) She can't listen to music because her radio is broken. 11) Can you give me your rubber, please? 12) It is raining so we can't go to the park.

My family's Likes and Dislikes

1) Yes, he does. 2) He likes potatoes, carrots and broccoli. 3) No, he doesn't. 4) They both like chicken. 5) The writer likes tea. 6) No, he doesn't. 7) He doesn't like pasta or broccoli. 8) No, she doesn't.

Like/Don't Like Speaking Practice

1) Do you like learning English? 2) What food do you like? 3) What drink do you like? 4) Where do you like best in this country? 5) Where do you like best in your country? 6) Do you like singing and dancing? 7) What sports do you like? 8) Do you like your home? 9) Do you like your town? 10) What TV programmes do you like? 11) What music do you like? 12) Why do you like your friends? 13) Do you like cats or dogs? 14) What transport do you like?

Common Mistakes: Like/don't like

1) I like my friend 2) Steve doesn't like his house. 3) We like cats and dogs. 4) Do you like cooking? 5) She doesn't like going to the gym. 6) What food do you like? 7) Does he like going to the park? 8) Peter and John like eating food. 9) We don't like the new restaurant. 10) My friend likes going shopping. 11) What colour does he like? 12) Why don't you like meeting me for a coffee?

Present Simple

1) likes 2) goes 3) watch 4) take 5) doesn't swim 6) drinks 7) play 8) starts 9) leave 10) look 11) doesn't run 12) works 13) cooks 14) love 15) call 16) don't drive

Derek's Day

1) He wakes up at 7am. 2) He eats toast with a little butter. 3) He brushes his teeth at 7:30. 4) He takes the bus for 20 minutes. 5) His college starts at 9:30. 6) He arrives home at 4:30. 7) He cooks rice or pasta and meat. 8) He sleeps at 11pm.

Present Simple Speaking Practice

1) What do you do on Saturdays? 2) What do you do on Sundays? 3) What time do you get up every morning? 4) What do you usually eat for breakfast? 5) What time do you leave your house? 6) How often do you take a bus? 7) What do you eat for lunch? 8) When do you go shopping? 9) What do you usually eat for dinner? 10) When do you watch TV? 11) What do you usually drink? 12) How do you relax? 13) How often do you clean your house? 14) What time do you go to bed?

Danny's Day

1) He wakes up at 6:30. 2) He eats a slice of toast. 3) He takes a shower at about 7am. 4) He takes the train to work. 5) He starts work at 9am. 6) He starts work at 1:30. 7) He gets home at 6pm. 8) He cooks dinner at 6:30. 9) He watches TV for an hour. 10) He sleeps at 11:30pm.

Present Simple Errors

1) I go to the park every day. 2) Sarah watches TV every night. 3) They study English at the college. 4) Do you brush your teeth every day? 5) He does not swim in the pool every summer.

6) My friend visits me every evening. 7) What time do you usually get up in the morning? 8) He listens to the radio at home. 9) What time does the shop open? 10) I like my job very much. 11) Does he like playing football? 12) My cat plays in the garden at night.

Present Continuous

1) is sleeping 2) are watching 3) is laughing 4) is working 5) are…doing 6) are meeting 7) are living 8) am not drinking 9) are…going 10) isn't working 11) is running 12) isn't shining 13) is raining 14) isn't working 15) is growing 16) is ringing 17) aren't running 18) is playing

Present Continuous Speaking Practice

1) What are you doing now? 2) Where are you going at the weekend? 3) Where are you studying now? 4) Who are you meeting after the lesson? 5) What is your friend doing at the moment? 6) Where are you going for your next trip? 7) Where is your friend living now? 8) What are you eating and drinking tonight? 9) Are you studying anything at the moment? 10) Are you watching TV tonight? 11) Is it raining tomorrow? 12) Are you enjoying your English lessons?

Common Mistakes – Present Continuous

1) John and Jill are swimming in the sea. 2) Mike is not reading a book at the moment. 3) They are watching TV in the living room. 4) They are running in the park. 5) I am not studying English now. 6) Is she calling her friend now? 7) Adam is writing a letter now. 8) Ann is relaxing on the sofa now. 9) She is learning English at school now. 10) Are you speaking to me? 11) I can't talk because I am working now. 12) She is not cooking dinner now.

Past Regular

1) played 2) watched 3) cooked 4) visited 5) washed 6) relaxed 7) cleaned 8) studied 9) copied 10) started 11) helped 12) called

1) cooked 2) enjoyed 3) Did…call 4) didn't work 5) danced 6) watched 7) stayed 8) didn't visit 9) smiled 10) didn't clean 11) relaxed 12) Did…jump

Dahira's Dinner

Mary <u>called</u> her friend Dahira on Friday and <u>visited</u> her in her flat last weekend. Dahira <u>cooked</u> dinner. She <u>cooked</u> roast chicken and potatoes. Mary <u>liked</u> the chicken but she <u>didn't like</u> the potatoes. They <u>talked</u> for a long time at the dinner table. They <u>talked</u> about work and their boyfriends. Both of the <u>cleaned</u> the dirty dishes and glasses in the sink. After the meal Mary and Dahira <u>listened</u> to pop music. Dahira <u>danced</u> but Mary <u>didn't</u>. Then they <u>relaxed</u> on the sofa and <u>watched</u> TV. They <u>watched</u> a Japanese film. Mary <u>stayed</u> for four hours at Dahira's home. They both <u>enjoyed</u> the evening very much.

1) 17 2) 13 3) She cooked roast chicken and potatoes. 4) No, she didn't. 5) They talked about work and their boyfriends. 6) The cleaned the dirty dishes and glasses. 7) No, she didn't. 8) They listened to pop music. 9) She stayed there for 4 hours. 10) Yes, they did.

Past Regular Speaking Practice

1) Who did you call last week? 2) Who did you visit last weekend? 3) Where did you travel last year? 4) When did you clean your home? 5) What did you study in your lesson? 6) Where did you walk last week? 7) Did you play a game last week? 8) What did you cook at the weekend? 9) Did you listen to music last week? 10) What did you watch on TV? 11) Did you enjoy your weekend? 12) How did you relax yesterday?

Common Mistakes - Past Tense Regular

1) He played football in the park. 2) Did he watch a film on TV? 3) My friend didn't visit me last weekend. 4) Bill listened to music yesterday. 5) I cooked a delicious meal for my family. 6) We studied very hard at college. 7) Adam didn't relax at home because he was busy. 8) Did you call your brother yesterday? 9) What time did the lesson start? 10) Did you wash your clothes? 11) My friend called me last night. 12) I cleaned my house because it was dirty.

Be Verb Past: Positive

1) was 2) was 3) were 4) were 5) was 6) were 7) was 8) was 9) was 10) were 11) was 12) was 13) were 14) was 15) was 16) was 17) were 18) was 19) was 20) was

Be Verb Past: Negative

1) was not 2) were not 3) was not 4) was not 5) was not 6) was not 7) was not 8) was not 9) was not 10) were not 11) was not 12) was not 13) was not 14) was not 15) were not 16) were not 17) were not 18) were not 19) was not 20) were not

Was/Were Speaking Practice

1) How was the weather yesterday? 2) Where were you last week? 3) Were you at home last weekend? 4) What was your dinner yesterday? 5) Who was your teacher at school? 6) Were you a good student at school? 7) Were you late for your English lesson last week? 8) Were you happy or sad last week? 9) How long were you in your last home? 10) Where was your last trip? 11) What was your happiest memory from last year? 12) What were your friends' names in your country?

Common Mistakes – Was/Were

1) We were not happy yesterday. 2) Where were you yesterday? 3) She was not in the gym when I went. 4) What was your favourite food as a child? 5) Why weren't you at school yesterday? 6) My trousers were clean. 7) Were you in the library yesterday? 8) I was sad that I couldn't see you. 9) I am sorry I was late for college yesterday. 10) Who was he with last week? 11) We were very tired after the lesson. 12) Were Peter and John happy at the party?

Past Irregular

go>went, eat>ate, drink>drank, meet>met, see>saw, have>had, make>made, do>did, buy>bought, pay>paid, stand>stood, wake>woke, write>wrote, speak>spoke, leave>left, take>took, can>could, run>ran, sing>sang, begin>began, read>read, sleep>slept, put>put

Past Irregular

Verb	Past	Verb	Past	Verb	Past	Verb	Past
Begin	*Began*	Go	*Went*	Meet	*Met*	Sleep	*Slept*
Buy	*Bought*	Have	*Had*	Pay	*Paid*	Speak	*Spoke*
Can	*Could*	Is	*Was/were*	Read	*Read*	Stand	*Stood*
Do	*Did*	Know	*Knew*	Run	*Ran*	Take	*Took*
Drink	*Drank*	Leave	*Left*	See	*Saw*	Wake	*Woke*
Eat	*Ate*	Make	*Made*	Sing	*Sang*	Write	*Wrote*

1) did 2) slept 3) wrote 4) spoke 5) ate 6) drank 7) bought 8) met 9) saw 10) took 11) had 12) paid 13) went 14) ran

William's Weekend

Last weekend William <u>took</u> the train to Bristol to meet his friend Gary. He <u>met</u> his friend Saturday at 1pm at the station. They <u>went</u> to the park together for a picnic. After lunch they <u>played</u> football and then <u>walked</u> by the river. In the evening they <u>went</u> to a restaurant. William <u>ate</u> chicken and Gary <u>ate</u> beef. They both <u>drank</u> beer. Gary <u>paid</u> the bill and they <u>went</u> home and <u>saw</u> a film.

On Sunday they <u>woke up</u> at 8am and <u>ran</u> in the park for an hour. They <u>came</u> home and <u>took</u> a shower. They <u>went</u> shopping. Gary <u>bought</u> food for lunch. After lunch they <u>said</u> goodbye and William <u>took</u> the train home.

1) 20. 2) 13 3) He went to Bristol. 4) They met at 1pm. 5) They ate chicken and beef. 6) They saw a film. 7) They woke up at 8am. 8) They ran for an hour. 9) He bought food for lunch. 10) He went home.

Past Irregular Speaking Practice

1) What did you do last week? 2) Who did you meet last weekend? 3) Where did you go last year? 4) What did you eat and drink last night? 5) What job did you do in your country? 6) Where did you live as a child? 7) When did you take a bus last? 8) Where is the best place you went last year? 9) What book did you read last? 10) When did you sing or dance last? 11) What did you buy last week? 12) What time did you wake up this morning?

Common Mistakes – Past Tense Irregular

1) I read a book last night. 2) Did Tom go to the gym yesterday? 3) He took the train to his office. 4) Did you meet your friend in the supermarket? 5) Peter ate delicious food yesterday. 6) Susan didn't drink coffee in the café. 7) We left the college very late last night. 8) Mike read

a book at school. 9) She bought some broccoli from the shop. 10) Did you speak with your parents yesterday? 11) Mary didn't wake up very early this morning. 12) I could play the piano when I was five years old.

Question Forms

1) Where are you from? 2) Where do you live now? 3) What is your hobby? 4) How often do you play? 5) Are you married? 6) Do you have any children? 7) How old are they? 8) What does your wife do? 9) Does she like her job? 10) How often does she work?

Speaking Practice:

1) Where do you live? 2) Do you like your area? 3) Where did you live before? 4) When were you born? 5) Where were you born? 6) What do you do? 7) How do you get to college? 8) Are you married? 9) Do you have any children? 10) How many brothers and sisters do you have? 11) Who do you like best in your family? 12) Who is your best friend? 13) What is your hobby? 14) How often do you exercise? 15) What did you do last weekend? 16) Who did you meet last weekend?

Future Plans – "going to"

Positive +	Negative -	Question ?
I am going to…	I am not going to…	Am I going to…?
You are going to…	You are not going to…	Are you going to…?
He is going to…	He is not going to…	Is he going to…?
She is going to…	She is not going to…	Is she going to…?
It is going to…	It is not going to…	Is it going to…?
We are going to…	We are not going to…	Are we going to…?
They are going to…	They are not going to…	Are they going to…?

1) watch 2) cook 3) buy 4) run 5) stay 6) play 7) visit 8) clean 9) call 10) drink 11) go 12) go

William's Weekend Work

1) He is a waiter. 2) He works in a restaurant in Cardiff. 3) He is going to start at 5pm. 4) He is going to prepare the tables. 5) He is going to work for 7 hours. 6) He is going to work at 11am. 7) He is going to serve lunch. 8) He is going to work 7 hours. 9) He is going to finish at 6pm. 10) He is going to go home by bus/He is going to take the bus.

Speaking Practice

1) What are you going to do after the lesson? 2) What are you going to do tonight? 3) What are you going to do at the weekend? 4) What are you going to eat and drink for dinner? 5) What time are you going to go to bed tonight? 6) What time are you going to get out of bed tomorrow? 7) What are you going to do next year? 8) When are you going to go shopping next? 9) Which friend are you going to meet next? 10) What are you going to wear at the weekend? 11) Where are you going to live in the future? 12) What job are you going to do in the future?

Common Mistakes – Going to

1) Are you going to meet your friend? 2) They are going to watch TV tonight. 3) I am going to drink a cup of tea. 4) Sarah is not going to read a book. 5) They are going to eat in a restaurant. 6) Michael is not going to climb a mountain at the weekend. 7) Are you going to play football? 8) Lisa is going to take a bus to go to work. 9) I am sad because my friend is going to live in the USA. 10) Mary is going to play tennis with his friend. 11) I am going to call my friend tonight. 12) Are you going to work tomorrow?

List of Irregular Verbs

Infinitive	Past
Be	Was/were
Begin	Began
Break	Broke
Bring	Brought
Build	Built
Buy	Bought
Can	Could
Catch	Caught
Come	Came
Cost	Cost
Cut	Cut
Do	Did
Drink	Drank
Drive	Drove
Eat	Ate
Grow	Grew
Fall	Fell
Feel	Felt
Find	Found
Fly	Flew
Forget	Forgot
Get	Got
Give	Gave
Go	Went
Have	Had
Hear	Heard
Hurt	Hurt
Know	Knew

Infinitive	Past
Learn	Learnt
Leave	Left
Lose	Lost
Make	Made
Meet	Met
Pay	Paid
Put	Put
Read	Read
Ride	Rode
Ring	Rang
Run	Ran
Say	Said
See	Saw
Send	Sent
Sing	Sang
Sit	Sat
Sleep	Slept
Speak	Spoke
Spend	Spent
Swim	Swam
Take	Took
Teach	Taught
Tell	Told
Think	Thought
Wake	Woke
Wear	Wore
Win	Won
Write	Wrote

Milton Keynes UK
Ingram Content Group UK Ltd.
UKHW051811110624
443890UK00002B/7

9 798543 021309